In the Summer

by Cameron Macintosh

OXFORD
UNIVERSITY PRESS
AUSTRALIA & NEW ZEALAND

In summer, it can be hot. It can be hard just to keep cool.

The bright sun can scorch the land.
The soil is hard and can crack.

In summer, we can get sunburn.

It's best not to go out for too long.

It's good to have a hat on if you go out.

A hat helps to keep the sun off.

At night, the sun is down. It can still be hot.

In summer, it can be hard to get to sleep.

This summer was hot. Lots of kids went to the pool.

They said that they felt much cooler at the pool.

This summer, the garden went brown.

The flowers were drooping.

This summer, it did not rain.

We kept the ferns wet and
under shelter.

Will it be so hot next summer?